The Complete Guide to Chapter 7 Bankruptcy

A Roadmap for Financial Recovery

Peter J. Lamont, Esq.

First Edition published by Law Offices of Peter J. Lamont 2023

Copyright © 2023 by Peter J. Lamont, Esq.

All rights reserved. No part of this publication may be reproduced, stored or transmitted in any form or by any means, electronic, mechanical, photocopying, recording, scanning, or otherwise without written permission from the publisher. It is illegal to copy this book, post it to a website, or distribute it by any other means without permission.

Peter J. Lamont, Esq. asserts the moral right to be identified as the author of this work.

Peter J. Lamont, Esq. has no responsibility for the persistence or accuracy of URLs for external or third-party Internet Websites referred to in this publication and does not guarantee that any content on such Websites is, or will remain, accurate or appropriate.

Designations used by companies to distinguish their products are often claimed as trademarks. All brand names and product names used in this book and on its cover are trade names, service marks, trademarks and registered trademarks of their respective owners. The publishers and the book are not associated with any product or vendor mentioned in this book. None of the companies referenced within the book have endorsed the book.

First Edition

Legal Disclaimer

This book, written by an attorney, is intended to provide general information and an overview of bankruptcy, with a specific focus on Chapter 7 bankruptcy. While every effort has been made to ensure the accuracy and completeness of the information contained herein, it is important to understand that this book does not constitute legal advice, nor does it establish an attorney-client relationship between the author and the reader.

Bankruptcy law is complex and subject to change, and the information provided in this book may not reflect the most recent legal developments or be applicable to your specific circumstances. Every individual's financial situation is unique, and the outcome of any bankruptcy case depends on various factors, including jurisdiction, the specific facts of the case, and the applicable laws and regulations.

Readers should not act or refrain from acting based on the information provided in this book without first seeking the advice of competent legal counsel licensed to practice in their jurisdiction. No representation or warranty, express or implied, is made as to the accuracy, reliability, or completeness of the information contained in this book, and the author expressly disclaims any liability for any errors or omissions in the content.

By reading this book, you acknowledge and agree that neither the author nor the publisher shall be held responsible or liable for any claims, damages, losses, or expenses, whether direct or indirect, consequential or incidental, that may result from your reliance on the information provided in this book or any actions taken or not taken based on such information.

The author and publisher specifically disclaim any responsibility for any liability, loss, or risk, personal or otherwise, which is incurred as a consequence, directly or indirectly, of the use and application of any of the contents of this book.

Table of contents

Introduction	7
The Four Types of Bankruptcy	9
What is Chapter 7 Bankruptcy?	14
You Are Not Alone	18
12 Bankruptcy Myths	22
The "Means" Test	26
Hiring a Bankruptcy Attorney	30
Preparing to File the Petition	34
The Chapter 7 Petition	39
Chapter 7 Bankruptcy Process	43
The Automatic Stay	47
Creditor Meeting (341 Hearing)	51
Exemptions	55
Reaffirming Debt	62
Debt Management Courses	66
Discharge	70
Life After Bankruptcy	74

CHAPTER 1

Introduction

> ❝ *Anybody who knows about capitalism knows that bankruptcy is an essential part of capitalism." -Joseph Stiglitz*

Introduction to Chapter 7 Bankruptcy

Bankruptcy is a word that often elicits fear, confusion, and a sense of failure in the minds of many. Despite its intimidating reputation, bankruptcy is a legal tool designed to relieve individuals and businesses overwhelmed by debt. It is a complex and intricate process, and as such, it is often misunderstood or clouded by misconceptions. That is precisely where "The Complete Guide to Chapter 7 Bankruptcy: A Roadmap for Financial Recovery" comes in.

This book aims to demystify the subject of bankruptcy by providing a comprehensive overview of the process, addressing common misconceptions, and presenting the pros and cons of each available option. Our objective is to empower you, the reader, with accurate and up-to-date information to help you make informed decisions about your financial future.

Bankruptcy is not a one-size-fits-all solution, and deciding whether or not it's the right path for you requires a careful evaluation of your individual circumstances. This book will guide you through the process of Chapter 7 bankruptcy, the key players involved, and the steps to take if you choose to embark on this journey. Additionally, we will discuss the potential consequences of filing for bankruptcy, including the impact on your credit and your long-term financial health.

As you navigate the pages of this book, I hope that you will gain a better understanding of the complexities of bankruptcy and how it may or may not be the best solution for your financial situation. By dispelling myths and providing a clear picture of the bankruptcy process, I aim to remove the stigma that often surrounds this topic and help you approach it with confidence and clarity.

Whether you are considering filing for bankruptcy or simply seeking to understand the topic better, "The Complete Guide to Chapter 7 Bankruptcy: A Roadmap for Financial Recovery" is a valuable resource, offering expert advice and insight into this often misunderstood area of finance.

CHAPTER 2

The Four Types of Bankruptcy

> **66** *Capitalism without bankruptcy is like Christianity without hell.* ” - *Frank Borman*

Understanding the Bankruptcy Code

Bankruptcy, a complex legal process designed to assist individuals and businesses struggling with debt, is divided into four distinct chapters, each tailored to address specific financial situations. While this book is about Chapter 7 bankruptcy, it may be helpful for you to have an overview of the different types of bankruptcy available.

A Breakdown of the Four Types of Bankruptcy

Each chapter of bankruptcy is designed to address specific financial situations and provide tailored solutions to help debtors regain control of their finances. This chapter will provide a comprehensive breakdown of the four primary types of bankruptcy—Chapter 7, Chapter 9, Chapter 11, and Chapter 13—highlighting their key features, eligibility criteria, and the intended beneficiaries.

Chapter 7 Bankruptcy: Liquidation

Chapter 7 bankruptcy, commonly referred to as "liquidation" bankruptcy, is designed for individuals who are unable to repay their debts. This type of bankruptcy allows debtors to discharge most of their unsecured debts by liquidating their non-exempt assets under the supervision of a court-appointed trustee. The proceeds from the sale of these assets are then used to repay creditors. Once the liquidation process is complete, most remaining unsecured debts are discharged, giving the debtor a fresh financial start.

Eligibility for Chapter 7 bankruptcy is determined through a "means test," which evaluates the debtor's income and expenses to ascertain whether they qualify for this form of relief or if they should pursue a Chapter 13 repayment plan. While Chapter 7 can provide significant debt relief, it is important to note that some debts, such as student loans, child support, alimony, and certain tax debts, are generally not dischargeable.

Chapter 9 Bankruptcy: Municipal Bankruptcy

Chapter 9 bankruptcy is a specialized form of bankruptcy reserved for municipalities, such as cities, towns, counties, and other governmental entities that are unable to meet their financial obligations. This type of bankruptcy allows municipalities to reorganize their debts and develop a repayment plan under the protection of the bankruptcy court. Chapter 9 is unique in that it does not involve liquidating assets, nor does it allow creditors to seize municipal assets to repay debts.

Eligibility for Chapter 9 bankruptcy is limited to municipalities that are specifically authorized to file for bankruptcy under state law. Additionally, the municipality must be insolvent, must have attempted to negotiate with its creditors, and must have a feasible plan for adjusting its debts.

Chapter 11 Bankruptcy: Reorganization

Chapter 11 bankruptcy, often associated with businesses, is a reorganization process that allows corporations, partnerships, and even some individuals to restructure their debts while continuing to operate. Under Chapter 11, the debtor, referred to as the "debtor in possession," remains in control of their business and assets while working to develop a reorganization plan that outlines how their debts will be repaid.

The reorganization plan must be approved by the bankruptcy court and most of the debtor's creditors. Once approved, the debtor is bound to follow the plan's terms, making payments to creditors according to the agreed-upon schedule. Chapter 11 bankruptcy can provide businesses with the opportunity to restructure their debts, renegotiate contracts, and emerge from bankruptcy as a stronger, more financially stable entity.

Chapter 13 Bankruptcy: Wage Earner's Plan

Chapter 13 bankruptcy, also known as a "wage earner's plan," is designed for individuals with a regular source of income who want to repay their debts over time while retaining their assets. Under Chapter 13, the debtor proposes a repayment plan, usually spanning three to five years, which details how their debts will be repaid using their disposable income.

Eligibility for Chapter 13 bankruptcy is contingent on the debtor's income and debt levels. There are specific debt limits for unsecured and secured debts that the debtor must not exceed to qualify for Chapter 13 Additionally, the debtor must demonstrate a regular income source that can support the proposed repayment plan.

Once the bankruptcy court confirms the repayment plan, the debtor makes payments to a court-appointed trustee, who distributes the funds to the creditors. Upon successfully completing the repayment plan, the debtor receives a discharge for any remaining eligible unsecured debts. Chapter 13 bankruptcy can be an attractive option for individuals seeking to protect their assets, such as a home or vehicle while working to repay their debts over an extended period.

Summary

Bankruptcy is a vital tool for individuals and businesses grappling with overwhelming debt, offering a path toward financial recovery and a fresh start. This book primarily focuses on Chapter 7 bankruptcy; however, it is important to be aware of the other available bankruptcy chapters to make an informed decision about your financial future.

By providing an overview of Chapter 7, Chapter 9, Chapter 11, and Chapter 13 bankruptcy, this book aims to empower you with the knowledge necessary to navigate the complexities of the bankruptcy process and choose the most suitable form of relief for your specific circumstances. As you explore the intricacies of Chapter 7 bankruptcy, remember that understanding the broader context and alternatives will help you make the best possible decision and set you on the path to reclaiming control over your financial life.

CHAPTER 3

What is Chapter 7 Bankruptcy?

66 *Bankruptcy is a serious decision that people have to make." - Herb Kohl*

The Basics

Before delving into the intricacies of Chapter 7 bankruptcy, it is imperative to establish a solid foundation of knowledge regarding its definition and its distinction from other types of bankruptcy. As one of the most prevalent forms of bankruptcy in the United States, Chapter 7 serves as a financial lifeline for individuals who are incapable of repaying their mounting debts. To better understand the inner workings of Chapter 7 bankruptcy, this chapter will present a comprehensive overview, detailing its eligibility criteria, the steps involved in the filing process, and the broader implications it has on your financial circumstances.

Understanding Bankruptcy and Chapter 7's Distinct Features

Bankruptcy is a legal process that allows individuals to eliminate or restructure their debts under the protection of federal bankruptcy courts. As discussed in Chapter 2, there are several types of bankruptcy, each tailored to specific situations and financial conditions. Among these, Chapter 7 bankruptcy is the most commonly filed form of consumer bankruptcy.

Unlike Chapter 13, which involves the restructuring of debts and the creation of a repayment plan, Chapter 7 focuses on liquidating the debtor's non-exempt assets to pay off creditors. This distinction is crucial because, in Chapter 7, the debtor is not required to repay any remaining unsecured debts after the liquidation process is completed. In contrast, Chapter 13 requires a commitment to a repayment plan over a specified period.

Chapter 7 Overview

To be eligible for Chapter 7 bankruptcy, you must pass the "means test," which compares your income to the state median income. If your income is below the state median, you are eligible for Chapter 7 bankruptcy. If your income is above the state median, you may still be eligible if you can show that you do not have enough disposable income to pay off your debts.

Once you file for Chapter 7 bankruptcy, an automatic stay goes into effect, which stops all collection activities, including lawsuits, wage garnishments, and creditor harassment. The bankruptcy court appoints a trustee to oversee your case and sell your non-exempt assets. You must provide the trustee with a list of all your debts, assets, income, and expenses.

In most cases, you can discharge all your unsecured debts, such as credit card debt, medical bills, and personal loans. However, some debts cannot be discharged, such as student loans, taxes, and child support payments.

After your debts are discharged, you can start rebuilding your credit by opening new credit accounts and making timely payments. Although a Chapter 7 bankruptcy will remain on your credit report for up to ten years, you can still achieve a good credit score by using credit responsibly and avoiding late payments and defaults.

In the following chapters, we will explore the various aspects of Chapter 7 bankruptcy in greater depth. We will discuss the eligibility criteria that debtors must meet to qualify for Chapter 7, as well as the filing process, which involves submitting a petition to the bankruptcy court and working with a court-appointed trustee. Furthermore, we will examine the broader effects that filing for Chapter 7 bankruptcy can have on your financial situation, including the impact on your credit score and the types of debts that can and cannot be discharged.

Summary

By providing a thorough overview of Chapter 7 bankruptcy, this chapter seeks to equip you with the knowledge necessary to determine whether this form of debt relief is the right choice for you. With a clear understanding of the eligibility requirements, filing process, and potential outcomes, you can make an informed decision about your financial future and take the first steps toward recovery.

CHAPTER 4

You Are Not Alone

66 *Don' t ever lose hope. Even when life seems bleak and hopeless, know that you are not alone." - Nancy Reagan*

The Same Boat

So many people are in the same boat. In the face of financial hardship, it is natural to feel isolated, overwhelmed, and even ashamed. However, it is crucial to understand that you are not alone in your struggle with debt. Millions of people find themselves in similar situations, and for many, filing for bankruptcy becomes an essential step toward financial recovery. This chapter will explore the prevalence of bankruptcy, the external factors contributing to financial distress, and the importance of overcoming the stigma associated with bankruptcy to regain control of your financial life.

The Prevalence of Bankruptcy

Bankruptcy is more common than many people realize. According to data from the American Bankruptcy Institute, hundreds of thousands of individuals and businesses file for bankruptcy yearly in the United States. In fact, according to statistics released by the Administrative Office of the U.S. Courts, the annual bankruptcy filings totaled 383,810, based on a 12-month cycle ending in September 2022.

Although the number of filings can fluctuate due to economic conditions, the fact remains that a significant number of people experience financial hardship and turn to bankruptcy as a viable solution.

It is essential to recognize that financial difficulties can affect people from all walks of life, regardless of their background, profession, or social status. From ordinary individuals and small business owners to celebrities and large corporations, many have found themselves in need of bankruptcy protection to restructure or eliminate their debts.

External Factors and Financial Hardship

Financial difficulties can arise for various reasons, often due to circumstances beyond an individual's control. Economic downturns, job loss, medical emergencies, divorce, and other unforeseen events can all contribute to mounting debt and financial instability. It is important to remember that good people can find themselves in difficult financial situations through no fault of their own.

Understanding that external factors often play a significant role in financial hardship can help alleviate feelings of shame or guilt that may be associated with bankruptcy. Rather than viewing bankruptcy as a personal failure, it is helpful to consider it a legal tool designed to assist individuals and businesses in recovering from financial setbacks.

Overcoming the Stigma of Bankruptcy

Despite its prevalence and legitimate purpose, bankruptcy still carries a social stigma for many people. This perception can make it difficult for individuals to seek the help they need or openly discuss their financial struggles. It is essential to challenge and overcome this stigma to access the support and resources necessary to regain control of your financial life.

One way to combat the stigma of bankruptcy is to focus on its purpose as a fresh start and a pathway toward financial recovery. Bankruptcy laws were designed to help individuals and businesses regain their financial footing, not as a punishment for those facing debt. Embracing this perspective can empower you to view bankruptcy as a proactive step towards rebuilding your financial future rather than a source of shame or embarrassment.

Another crucial aspect of overcoming the stigma of bankruptcy is fostering open and honest conversations about financial difficulties. By sharing your experiences and acknowledging the challenges faced by millions of others, you can help break down the barriers that often surround discussions about debt and bankruptcy.

Summary

In the face of financial hardship, it is essential to remember that you are not alone. Bankruptcy is a common and legitimate solution for individuals and businesses experiencing financial difficulties, often due to circumstances beyond their control. By recognizing the prevalence of bankruptcy, understanding the external factors that contribute to financial distress, and overcoming the stigma associated with bankruptcy, you can take the necessary steps toward financial recovery with confidence and hope. Remember, seeking help and pursuing bankruptcy when necessary is not a sign of failure but rather a testament to your resilience and determination to reclaim control over your financial life.

CHAPTER 5

---

12 Bankruptcy Myths

❝ *The great enemy of the truth is very often not the lie, deliberate, contrived and dishonest, but the myth, persistent, persuasive and unrealistic." - John F. Kennedy*

12 Myths (and Truths) of Chapter 7 Bankruptcy

Bankruptcy is a complex and often misunderstood area of law that can be shrouded in misconceptions and myths. These myths, which can lead to confusion and fear, might prevent individuals from seeking the help they need to regain control of their financial lives. This chapter aims to dispel 12 common myths about bankruptcy by presenting the facts and revealing the truth behind each one. By debunking these myths, we hope to provide clarity and empower those facing financial challenges to make informed decisions about whether bankruptcy is the right solution for their unique circumstances.

1. **Myth:** You will lose all your assets in Chapter 7 bankruptcy. **Truth:** While some assets may be liquidated to repay creditors, many assets are exempt from liquidation. Exemptions vary by state but often include essentials such as clothing, furniture, and a certain amount of equity in a home or vehicle.

2. **Myth:** Chapter 7 bankruptcy permanently ruins your credit. **Truth:** A Chapter 7 bankruptcy will stay on your credit report for ten years, but your credit score can begin to improve well before that. By establishing good financial habits and responsibly using credit, you can rebuild your credit over time.

3. **Myth:** Filing for Chapter 7 bankruptcy is a sign of financial irresponsibility. **Truth:** Many people face bankruptcy due to unforeseen circumstances, such as medical expenses, job loss, or divorce. Bankruptcy is a legal tool designed to relieve those facing overwhelming debt.

4. **Myth:** You can't get a loan or credit card after filing for Chapter 7 bankruptcy. **Truth**: While it may be more challenging to obtain credit initially, responsible financial behavior and rebuilding your credit can eventually lead to approval for loans or credit cards.

5. **Myth:** Bankruptcy wipes out all types of debt. **Truth:** Chapter 7 bankruptcy discharges many

types of debt, but certain obligations like student loans, alimony, child support, and some taxes remain.

6. **Myth:** You can only file for Chapter 7 bankruptcy once in your lifetime. **Truth:** There is no limit to the number of times you can file, but you must wait eight years after a previous Chapter 7 discharge to file again.

7. **Myth:** Filing for Chapter 7 bankruptcy means you're a failure. **Truth:** Bankruptcy is a legal process designed to help individuals and businesses regain control of their finances. It's a fresh start, not a mark of failure.

8. **Myth:** Chapter 7 bankruptcy is expensive and complicated. **Truth:** While there are costs associated with filing, they are typically much lower than the debt being discharged. Additionally, experienced bankruptcy attorneys can help guide you through the process.

9. **Myth:** Everyone will know you filed for bankruptcy. **Truth:** Bankruptcy filings are public records, but most people won't know unless you tell them or they actively search for the information.

10. **Myth:** Married couples must file for bankruptcy together. **Truth:** Married couples can choose to file jointly or separately, depending on their specific financial situation and goals.

11. **Myth:** Chapter 7 bankruptcy is the only option for individuals facing overwhelming debt. **Truth:** There are other bankruptcy options, such as Chapter 13, which

reorganizes debt into a manageable repayment plan. It's essential to consult with a bankruptcy attorney to determine the best course of action for your situation.

12. **Myth:** You can strategically run up debt before filing for Chapter 7 bankruptcy. **Truth:** Racking up debt to discharge it through bankruptcy is considered fraud and can result in criminal charges, denial of discharge, or other penalties.

Having dispelled the 12 most common myths and misconceptions about bankruptcy, it is now time to delve deeper into the intricacies of the bankruptcy process. This understanding will empower you to make informed decisions about your financial future. The following chapters will provide a comprehensive guide to the procedures involved and the essential factors to consider when navigating this complex legal landscape. As we transition from debunking myths to exploring the realities of bankruptcy, I aim to equip you with the knowledge and resources necessary to make the best possible choices for your unique situation, ultimately paving the way for a brighter financial future.

CHAPTER 6

The "Means" Test

❝ *It is said that the world is in a state of bankruptcy, that the world owes the world more than the world can pay."- Ralph Waldo Emerson*

Navigating the Means Test in Chapter 7 Bankruptcy

A critical aspect of the Chapter 7 bankruptcy process is the means test, a mechanism used to determine whether an individual qualifies for Chapter 7 relief or if they should pursue a Chapter 13 repayment plan instead. This chapter will provide an overview of the means test, explaining how it works, how it is calculated, and the consequences of not qualifying for Chapter 7 bankruptcy.

What is the Means Test?

The means test is a statutory requirement introduced by the Bankruptcy Abuse Prevention and Consumer Protection Act of 2005 (BAPCPA) to prevent individuals with sufficient income from discharging their debts through Chapter 7 bankruptcy. The primary purpose of the means test is to ensure that only those who genuinely cannot repay their debts have access to Chapter 7 relief.

How the Means Test Works

The means test is a two-step process that evaluates an individual's income and expenses to determine their eligibility for Chapter 7 bankruptcy.

Step 1: Median Income Comparison The first step of the means test involves comparing the debtor's average monthly income over the six months preceding the bankruptcy filing to the median income for a household of the same size in their state. If the debtor's income is below the median, they automatically qualify for Chapter 7 bankruptcy.

Step 2: Disposable Income Calculation If the debtor's income is above the state median, they proceed to the second step of the means test. This step involves calculating the debtor's disposable income by deducting certain allowable expenses from their monthly income, as outlined in the Internal Revenue Service's (IRS) National and Local Standards. Allowable expenses include housing, transportation, utilities, taxes, insurance, and other necessary costs. After deducting these expenses, the remaining disposable income is evaluated to determine if it is sufficient to repay a portion of the unsecured debt over a five-year period.

Consequences of Not Qualifying for Chapter 7 Bankruptcy

If the means test indicates that the debtor has enough disposable income to repay a portion of their unsecured debts, they will not qualify for Chapter 7 bankruptcy. In such cases, the debtor may consider filing for Chapter 13 bankruptcy instead, establishing a court-approved repayment plan lasting three to five years. Chapter 13 bankruptcy allows individuals to retain their assets while repaying their debts, making it a suitable alternative for those not qualifying for Chapter 7 relief.

It is important to note that failing the means test does not disqualify an individual from all bankruptcy relief; rather, it serves as a guide to determine the most appropriate form of bankruptcy based on their financial situation. Consulting with an experienced bankruptcy attorney can help individuals navigate the intricacies of the means test and explore other bankruptcy options if they do not qualify for Chapter 7.

Summary

The means test is the first step in the Chapter 7 bankruptcy process. By evaluating an individual's income and expenses, the means test ensures that Chapter 7 relief is reserved for those who genuinely cannot repay their debts. As you embark on the journey to financial recovery, understanding the role and implications of the means test is essential in determining whether Chapter 7 bankruptcy is a suitable option for your unique financial situation. Remember that the means test is just the beginning. Once eligibility is determined, you can proceed with the subsequent steps of the Chapter 7 bankruptcy process, working towards a fresh start and a renewed sense of financial stability.

CHAPTER 7

Hiring a Bankruptcy Attorney

66 *A lawyer who represents himself in court has a fool for a client."*

The Importance of Hiring a Bankruptcy Attorney for Your Chapter 7 Bankruptcy

As previously mentioned, filing for Chapter 7 bankruptcy can be a complex and daunting process involving numerous legal requirements, paperwork, and deadlines. While it is possible to file for bankruptcy on your own, known as filing "pro se," hiring a knowledgeable and experienced bankruptcy attorney can significantly increase your chances of a successful outcome.

Why Hiring a Bankruptcy Attorney is Crucial

Navigating the legal complexities of Chapter 7 bankruptcy can be challenging without professional assistance. Here are some reasons why hiring a bankruptcy attorney is essential:

1. **Expertise:** Bankruptcy attorneys have the knowledge and experience to handle your case effectively. They understand the intricacies of the bankruptcy code, the means test, and the specific requirements of your jurisdiction.

2. **Guidance:** A bankruptcy attorney can help you determine if Chapter 7 is the right choice for your financial situation, advise you on alternatives if necessary, and guide you through every step of the process, from filing the petition to attending the meeting of creditors and securing a discharge of your debts.

3. **Avoiding Mistakes:** Filing for bankruptcy involves extensive paperwork, and even minor errors can result in significant delays or even dismissal of your case. An attorney can help ensure that your petition and schedules are accurate, complete, and submitted on time.

4. **Protection from Creditors:** Once you hire a bankruptcy attorney, they can communicate with your creditors on your behalf, helping to end harassing phone calls and collection efforts.

Consequences of Not Hiring an Attorney

Attempting to file for Chapter 7 bankruptcy without the assistance of an attorney can lead to various negative consequences:

1. **Case Dismissal:** Failure to comply with the requirements of the bankruptcy process, such as missing deadlines, incomplete paperwork, or improper handling of assets, can result in the dismissal of your case without obtaining a discharge.

2. **Loss of Assets:** Without the guidance of an attorney, you may inadvertently fail to protect your assets from liquidation, resulting in the loss of property that you may have been able to retain with proper legal counsel.

3. **Denied Discharge:** If the court finds that you have committed fraud, failed to complete the required credit counseling or financial management courses, or otherwise violated the bankruptcy code, your discharge may be denied, leaving you responsible for your debts despite having gone through the bankruptcy process.

How a Bankruptcy Attorney Can Help

Hiring a bankruptcy attorney to handle your Chapter 7 bankruptcy can provide invaluable support and guidance throughout the process. From evaluating your financial situation and determining your eligibility for Chapter 7 to preparing and filing your petition, protecting your assets, and representing you in court, an attorney can help ensure that your bankruptcy case proceeds smoothly and efficiently.

In addition, a bankruptcy attorney can provide emotional support and reassurance during a challenging time, helping to alleviate the stress and uncertainty that often accompanies the bankruptcy process.

Summary

Filing for Chapter 7 bankruptcy is a complex process with potentially life-altering consequences. Hiring a knowledgeable and experienced bankruptcy attorney can significantly increase the likelihood of a successful outcome, ensuring you navigate the process effectively and secure the financial relief you need. While it may be tempting to try to handle your bankruptcy case on your own, the risks of doing so without professional assistance can be substantial. Engaging the services of a bankruptcy attorney is a wise investment in your financial future, providing the support and guidance necessary to help you regain control of your financial life and move forward confidently.

CHAPTER 8

Preparing to File the Petition

> **"** *By failing to prepare, you are preparing to fail."* — *Benjamin Franklin*

Gathering Essential Information for Your Attorney

Filing for Chapter 7 bankruptcy requires thorough preparation and attention to detail. One of the essential steps in this process is gathering the necessary information and documentation to present to your bankruptcy attorney prior to filing the petition.

Financial Records

Preparing to File the Petition   35

To accurately assess your financial situation and prepare the bankruptcy petition, your attorney will need access to various financial records. These records include:

1. **Income Documentation:** Provide pay stubs or other proof of income for the six months preceding the bankruptcy filing. This information is crucial for calculating the means test and determining your eligibility for Chapter 7 bankruptcy.

2. **Tax Returns:** Your attorney will need copies of your federal and state income tax returns for the last two years.

3. **Bank Statements:** Provide copies of your bank account statements for at least the last six months.

4. **Retirement Accounts:** Submit documentation for any retirement accounts you may have, including 401(k)s, IRAs, and pension plans.

5. **Real Estate and Vehicle Documentation:** Provide documents related to any real estate or vehicles you own, including deeds, titles, mortgages, and loan agreements.

Debts and Liabilities

A comprehensive list of all your debts and liabilities is essential for your attorney to prepare the bankruptcy schedules accurately. This list should include:

Credit Card Debts: Obtain statements or account summaries for all your credit card accounts.

2. **Loans:** Include information on any outstanding loans, such as personal loans, student loans, or payday loans.

3. **Medical Bills:** Compile records of any unpaid medical bills, including those from hospitals, doctors, or other healthcare providers.

4. **Taxes:** If you have outstanding tax liabilities, provide documentation from the Internal Revenue Service (IRS) or state tax agency.

5. **Child Support or Alimony:** Include any court orders or other documentation related to child support or alimony obligations.

6. **Lawsuits and Judgments:** Provide information on any pending lawsuits or judgments against you, including case numbers and the names of the parties involved.

Expenses and Living Costs

Your attorney will also need a detailed account of your monthly living expenses to prepare the bankruptcy schedules and calculate your disposable income. These expenses may include:

1. **Housing:** Rent or mortgage payments, property taxes, insurance, and utilities.

Preparing to File the Petition **37**

2. **Transportation:** Car payments, insurance, fuel, and maintenance costs.

3. **Food and Groceries:** The average monthly cost of food for your household.

4. **Clothing and Personal Care:** Expenses for clothing, grooming, and hygiene products.

5. **Medical and Dental Expenses:** Out-of-pocket costs for medical and dental care not covered by insurance.

6. **Childcare and Education:** Costs associated with childcare, tuition, or other educational expenses.

7. **Insurance:** Premiums for health, life, disability, and other insurance policies.

8. **Miscellaneous Expenses:** Any other monthly expenses, such as entertainment, memberships, or subscriptions.

Worksheets

Often, your bankruptcy attorney will provide you with a comprehensive worksheet to assist you in gathering the necessary documents and information before preparing the petition. This worksheet serves as a helpful tool in ensuring that you compile all the required financial records, debts, and expenses in an organized manner. By using this worksheet, you can simplify the process of preparing for your bankruptcy filing, reduce the risk of overlooking critical information, and ultimately facilitate a smoother and more efficient collaboration with your attorney.

Summary

Gathering the necessary information and documentation for your attorney is a crucial step in the Chapter 7 bankruptcy process. By providing accurate and complete records of your income, debts, and expenses, you can help ensure that your bankruptcy petition is prepared efficiently and accurately, increasing the likelihood of a successful outcome. Taking the time to compile this information before meeting with your attorney will not only streamline the process but also demonstrate your commitment to addressing your financial difficulties and achieving a fresh start.

CHAPTER 9

The Chapter 7 Petition

66 *The worst bankruptcy in the world is the person who has lost his enthusiasm." -William Howard Arnold*

The Bankruptcy Petition

The Chapter 7 bankruptcy petition is arguably the most crucial document in the bankruptcy process. It provides the court with an overview of your financial situation and serves as the foundation for your case. Preparing and filing the petition accurately and thoroughly ensures a smooth and successful bankruptcy process. This chapter will guide you through the steps involved in preparing and filing the Chapter 7 bankruptcy petition.

Preparing the Bankruptcy Petition

A Chapter 7 bankruptcy petition consists of numerous forms and schedules that detail your financial information, including assets, liabilities, income, and expenses. Your attorney will prepare the petition for you. the process of preparing the petition includes the following steps:

1. **Complete the Official Bankruptcy Forms:** The U.S. Bankruptcy Court provides a set of official forms that must be completed as part of your petition. These forms include the Voluntary Petition for Individuals Filing for Bankruptcy (Form 101), as well as a series of schedules (Forms 106A/B through 106J) that detail your assets, liabilities, income, expenses, and other financial information.

2. **Collect Supporting Documentation:** As discussed in Chapter 7, gather all necessary financial records, including income documentation, tax returns, bank statements, and information on debts and liabilities.

3. **Prepare a List of Creditors:** Compile a comprehensive list of all creditors, including their names, addresses, and the amount and nature of the debt owed.

4. **Complete the Means Test:** As outlined in Chapter 4, complete the means test to determine your eligibility for Chapter 7 bankruptcy.

5. **Complete the Credit Counseling Requirement:** Before filing for bankruptcy, you must complete a credit counseling course from an approved provider and submit the certificate of completion with your petition.

Filing the Bankruptcy Petition

Once the bankruptcy petition and all accompanying forms and schedules are complete, follow these steps to file your case:

1. **Assemble the Petition Package:** Compile the completed bankruptcy forms, schedules, and all required supporting documents into a single package. This package should include the Voluntary Petition, the completed schedules, the means test calculation, the credit counseling certificate, and any other required forms or documents.

2. **Submit the Petition to the Bankruptcy Court:** File the petition package with the U.S. Bankruptcy Court that serves your jurisdiction. This can be done electronically or in person, depending on the court's requirements.

3. **Pay the Filing Fee:** A filing fee is required to initiate your Chapter 7 bankruptcy case. As of September 2021, the fee is $338, though this amount may change over time. If you cannot afford to pay the fee in full, you can request to pay it in installments or apply for a waiver.

4. **Receive Your Case Number and Trustee Assignment:** Upon filing your petition, the court will assign a case number and a bankruptcy trustee to oversee your case. The trustee is responsible for reviewing your petition, verifying the information provided, and administering the bankruptcy estate.

Attend the Meeting of Creditors: Approximately 30 to 45 days after filing your petition, you must attend a meeting of creditors, also known as the 341 meeting. At this meeting, the trustee and any attending creditors can ask you questions about your financial situation and the information provided in your petition.

Summary

Preparing and filing the Chapter 7 bankruptcy petition is a critical step in the bankruptcy process, requiring meticulous attention to detail and accurate representation of your financial situation. By following the steps outlined in this chapter and working closely with your bankruptcy attorney, you can ensure that your petition is complete, accurate, and filed in a timely manner, setting the stage for a successful bankruptcy case and the opportunity for a fresh financial start.

CHAPTER 10

Chapter 7 Bankruptcy Process

> ❝ Slow down. Calm down. Don't worry. Don't hurry. Trust the process." – Alexandra Stoddard

The Chapter 7 Bankruptcy Process – From Filing to Discharge

Once you have filed your Chapter 7 bankruptcy petition, several important events and milestones will occur as your case progresses. Understanding each step in the process and knowing what to expect can help alleviate anxiety and ensure a smoother experience. Below we outline the key stages in the Chapter 7 bankruptcy process, from filing the petition to obtaining a discharge. We will go into greater detail about some of these events in separate chapters.

The Automatic Stay

Upon filing your bankruptcy petition, an automatic stay goes into effect, immediately halting collection efforts by your creditors. The stay provides temporary protection from:

1. Foreclosure or repossession actions.

2. Utility disconnections.

3. Wage garnishments.

4. Collection lawsuits.

5. Harassing phone calls and other communication from creditors.

The automatic stay remains in effect throughout the bankruptcy process unless a creditor successfully petitions the court to lift the stay for a specific reason.

The Meeting of Creditors (341 Meeting)

As mentioned in Chapter 7, the meeting of creditors takes place approximately 30 to 45 days after filing your petition. You must attend this meeting, where the bankruptcy trustee and any creditors who choose to participate can ask you questions about your financial situation and the information provided in your petition. The purpose of this meeting is to ensure that your petition is accurate and that you have disclosed all relevant information.

The Trustee's Review and Liquidation of Assets

The bankruptcy trustee assigned to your case will review your petition, verify the information provided, and determine whether any of your assets are non-exempt and subject to liquidation. The trustee may sell non-exempt assets to pay your creditors, but it is important to note that many Chapter 7 cases are "no-asset" cases, meaning all assets are protected, and no property is sold.

Financial Management Course

Before receiving a discharge, you must complete a debtor education course, also known as a financial management course, from an approved provider. This course will teach you valuable financial skills to help you manage your money and avoid future financial problems. Be sure to file the certificate of completion with the bankruptcy court.

Discharge of Debts

Approximately 60 to 90 days after the meeting of creditors, if you have met all the requirements and no objections have been raised, the bankruptcy court will issue a discharge order. This discharge eliminates your personal liability for most of your unsecured debts, such as credit card debts, medical bills, and personal loans. Some debts, like student loans, child support, and certain tax obligations, are typically not dischargeable.

Summary

The Chapter 7 bankruptcy process involves several key milestones, from the automatic stay and meeting of creditors to the trustee's review of assets and the ultimate discharge of eligible debts. Understanding each step in the process can help you navigate your bankruptcy case with confidence and set the stage for a fresh financial start. By working closely with your bankruptcy attorney and fulfilling your responsibilities throughout the process, you can maximize the benefits of Chapter 7 bankruptcy and put your financial troubles behind you.

CHAPTER 11

The Automatic Stay

66 *Medical debts are the number-one cause of bankruptcy in America." - Barbara Ehrenreich*

The Automatic Stay - A Lifeline During Your Bankruptcy

The automatic stay is a powerful aspect of the bankruptcy process that offers immediate relief to individuals and businesses filing for bankruptcy. This legal provision comes into effect when you file your bankruptcy petition and provides a temporary reprieve from creditor actions while your case is pending. This chapter will discuss the automatic stay in-depth, including its effects, limitations, and potential challenges.

Effects of the Automatic Stay

Upon filing your bankruptcy petition, the automatic stay offers immediate protection from various collection efforts and legal actions by your creditors, including:

1. **Collection Calls and Letters:** Creditors must cease all communication attempts, including phone calls, letters, and emails, demanding payment.

2. **Foreclosure Proceedings:** The automatic stay temporarily halts foreclosure actions on your home, giving you some breathing room to explore options for addressing your mortgage debt.

3. **Repossessions:** Creditors cannot repossess your car or other property during the automatic stay without first obtaining court permission.

4. **Wage Garnishments:** The automatic stay stops most wage garnishments, allowing you to receive your entire paycheck while your bankruptcy case is pending.

5. **Utility Disconnections:** Utility companies cannot disconnect your services for non-payment during the automatic stay.

6. **Evictions:** In some instances, the automatic stay can temporarily delay eviction proceedings, though this protection is limited.

Limitations of the Automatic Stay

While the automatic stay offers broad protection, it does not apply to all types of debts and legal actions. Some exceptions include:

1. **Child Support and Alimony:** The automatic stay does not stop the collection of child support or alimony obligations.

2. **Criminal Proceedings:** The automatic stay does not affect criminal proceedings or certain actions related to restitution or criminal penalties.

3. **Tax Proceedings:** Some tax collection actions, such as audits or tax assessments, may continue during the automatic stay, but the IRS and state tax agencies cannot seize your property or income.

Challenges to the Automatic Stay

Sometimes, a creditor may petition the court to lift the automatic stay. Common reasons for such requests include the following:

1. **Lack of Adequate Protection:** A secured creditor may argue that the value of their collateral (e.g., your home or car) declines during the automatic stay and that their interest is not adequately protected.

2. **Multiple Bankruptcy Filings:** If you have filed for bankruptcy multiple times in a short period, the automatic stay may be limited in duration, or a creditor

may argue that it should not apply due to potential abuse of the bankruptcy process.

3. **No Equity in Property:** If a creditor can demonstrate that you have no equity in a particular asset and that the asset is not necessary for an effective reorganization, the court may lift the automatic stay to allow the creditor to seize and sell the property.

The court will evaluate the merits of the creditor's request and may grant or deny the motion to lift the automatic stay.

Summary

The automatic stay is a powerful tool that offers immediate relief to debtors facing financial distress. By temporarily halting collection efforts and legal actions, the automatic stay provides an opportunity to regroup, assess your financial situation, and develop a strategy for moving forward. While the automatic stay has some limitations and can be challenged by creditors, it remains an essential lifeline for those seeking refuge from overwhelming debt and a fresh financial start through the bankruptcy process.

CHAPTER 12

Creditor Meeting (341 Hearing)

> 66 *Give me six hours to chop down a tree and I will spend the first four sharpening the axe."*
> — *Abraham Lincoln*

Navigating the 341 Hearing

The Meeting of Creditors, also known as the 341 Meeting, is a mandatory event in the bankruptcy process where you, the debtor, meet with the bankruptcy trustee and any creditors who choose to attend. The purpose of this meeting is to verify the information in your bankruptcy petition, ensure you have disclosed all relevant information, and allow creditors the opportunity to ask questions. This chapter will provide an in-depth look at the 341 Meeting, including its purpose, what to expect, and how to prepare for it.

Purpose of the Meeting of Creditors

The primary objectives of the 341 Meeting are to:

1. Confirm your identity and the accuracy of the information provided in your bankruptcy petition.

2. Ensure that you have disclosed all assets, liabilities, income, and expenses.

3. Allow the bankruptcy trustee and creditors to ask you questions regarding your financial situation and the information in your petition.

4. Provide creditors an opportunity to gather information that may be relevant to their claims or the administration of the bankruptcy estate.

What to Expect at the Meeting of Creditors

The 341 Meeting typically takes place approximately 30 to 45 days after filing your bankruptcy petition. It is important to note that the meeting is not held in a courtroom, and the bankruptcy judge is not present. Here's what you can expect:

1. **Location:** The meeting is usually held at the office of the U.S. Trustee, bankruptcy court, or another designated location.

Creditor Meeting (341 Hearing)   53

2. **Attendance:** You, the debtor, must attend the meeting, and your bankruptcy attorney will likely accompany you. Creditors may choose to attend, but their presence is not mandatory.

3. **Identification:** You must bring government-issued photo identification and proof of your Social Security number to the meeting.

4. **Sworn Testimony:** The bankruptcy trustee will place you under oath, and you will be required to provide truthful answers to the questions asked.

5. **Questions:** The trustee will ask questions about your financial situation, assets, liabilities, and any other relevant information in your bankruptcy petition. Creditors may also ask questions, but they are usually limited in scope and duration.

Preparing for the Meeting of Creditors

Preparing for the 341 Meeting can help ease anxiety and ensure a smoother experience. Here are some tips for getting ready:

1. **Review Your Bankruptcy Petition:** Go over your bankruptcy petition carefully with your attorney to refresh your memory on the details provided and ensure that you understand and can explain the information.

2.

Gather Required Documents: In addition to your identification and Social Security proof, you may need to provide additional documents requested by the trustee, such as recent pay stubs, bank statements, or tax returns.

3. **Practice Answering Questions:** Your attorney can help you prepare by reviewing potential questions that the trustee or creditors may ask, such as questions about your assets, debts, or reasons for filing bankruptcy.

4. **Dress Appropriately:** While there is no strict dress code for the 341 Meeting, dressing professionally and conservatively shows respect for the process and can make a positive impression on the trustee and creditors.

Summary

The Meeting of Creditors is a critical event in the bankruptcy process that allows the trustee and creditors to review and verify the information in your bankruptcy petition. By understanding the purpose of the 341 Meeting, knowing what to expect, and adequately preparing, you can approach the meeting with confidence and contribute to a smoother bankruptcy process. Your bankruptcy attorney will play a key role in guiding and supporting you throughout this important step on your journey toward financial recovery.

CHAPTER 13

Exemptions

66 *True nobility is exempt from fear" - Marcus Tullius Cicero*

Bankruptcy Exemptions – Protecting Your Assets

Bankruptcy exemptions can protect certain assets from being liquidated to pay your creditors. These exemptions allow you to retain specific assets, enabling you to maintain a basic standard of living and facilitating your financial recovery. In this chapter, we will discuss the concept of bankruptcy exemptions, the differences between federal and state exemptions, common types of exemptions, and the process for claiming them.

What are Bankruptcy Exemptions?

Bankruptcy exemptions are laws that protect specific property from being sold or seized to satisfy your debts during the bankruptcy process. These exemptions ensure you can retain a minimum level of assets necessary to rebuild your life after bankruptcy.

Federal vs. State Exemptions

Bankruptcy exemptions can be either federal or state-based. Each state has its own set of exemptions, and some states also allow you to choose between state and federal exemptions.

1. **Federal Exemptions:** These exemptions are provided by federal law and are available to debtors in all states. They include a range of property types, such as homestead, personal property, tools of the trade, and retirement accounts.

2. **State Exemptions:** State exemptions vary widely and may be more or less generous than federal exemptions. Some states have extensive lists of exemptions, while others provide only a few specific exemptions. In some cases, state exemptions may better suit your specific circumstances and protect more of your assets.

It is essential to consult with a bankruptcy attorney to determine which set of exemptions is most beneficial for your situation.

Common Types of Exemptions

While exemptions vary by jurisdiction, some common types of exemptions include:

1. **Homestead Exemption:** This exemption protects a certain amount of equity in your primary residence. The amount varies by state, with some states offering generous homestead exemptions and others providing more modest protection.

2. **Personal Property Exemption:** This exemption covers a variety of personal property, such as clothing, furniture, appliances, and other household items, up to a specified value.

3. **Vehicle Exemption:** This exemption protects a certain amount of equity in your primary vehicle, allowing you to keep your car or truck for transportation.

4. **Tools of the Trade Exemption:** This exemption protects tools, equipment, and other items necessary for your profession or trade up to a specified value.

5. **Retirement Accounts Exemption:** Most retirement accounts, such as 401(k)s, IRAs, and pension plans, are protected under federal law and exempt from liquidation in bankruptcy.

Claiming Exemptions

To claim exemptions in your bankruptcy case, you must:

1.

Identify the Exemptions: Work with your bankruptcy attorney to determine which set of exemptions (federal or state) is most advantageous for your situation and identify the specific exemptions that apply to your property.

2. **List Your Property:** In your bankruptcy petition, you must list all your property and assets, along with their estimated values.

3. **Specify the Exemptions:** For each item of property listed in your petition, you must specify the applicable exemption(s) and the corresponding exemption amount(s).

4. **File the Petition:** File your bankruptcy petition, including the Schedule C form, which lists your claimed exemptions, with the bankruptcy court.

It is essential to accurately list your property and apply the appropriate exemptions to protect your assets during the bankruptcy process.

New Jersey Specific Exemptions

The following are examples of some specific exemptions under New Jersey law:

Homestead Exemption: New Jersey does not have a specific homestead exemption. However, a debtor may use the wildcard exemption to protect some equity in their home.

Exemptions 59

Personal Property Exemption:

Clothing and household goods: 100% of the value of the debtor's clothing, household goods, and furnishings are exempt (N.J. Stat. Ann. § 2A:17-19).

- Jewelry: Up to $1,000 of the debtor's jewelry is exempt (N.J. Stat. Ann. § 2A:17-19).

- Health aids: Professionally prescribed health aids are exempt (N.J. Stat. Ann. § 2A:17-19).

Motor Vehicle Exemption: New Jersey does not have a specific motor vehicle exemption. However, a debtor may use the wildcard exemption to protect some equity in their vehicle.

Wildcard Exemption: New Jersey allows a wildcard exemption of up to $1,000 in value for any personal property (N.J. Stat. Ann. § 2A:17-19). This wildcard exemption can be applied to any personal property, including equity in a home or vehicle.

Tools of the Trade Exemption: Tools, implements, materials, or other personal property, up to $2,500 in value, are exempt if necessary for the debtor's profession or trade (N.J. Stat. Ann. § 2A:17-17).

Retirement Accounts Exemption:

- ERISA-qualified retirement plans, such as 401(k)s, 403(b)s, and pension plans, are exempt (N.J. Stat. Ann. §

25:2-1(b)).

- Traditional and Roth IRAs are exempt up to $1,283,025 (adjusted periodically for inflation) (N.J. Stat. Ann. § 25:2-1(b)).

- Public employee pension benefits are exempt (N.J. Stat. Ann. § 43:15A-53).

Insurance Benefits Exemption:

- Life insurance proceeds, if the policy's terms prohibit using them to pay creditors (N.J. Stat. Ann. § 17B:24-6).

- Disability or health benefits are exempt (N.J. Stat. Ann. § 17B:24-8).

- Annuity benefits are exempt up to $500 per month (N.J. Stat. Ann. § 17B:24-7).

Public Benefits Exemption:

- Unemployment compensation, workers' compensation, and other public assistance benefits are exempt (N.J. Stat. Ann. § 43:21-15).

- Social Security benefits are exempt (N.J. Stat. Ann. § 25:2-1(a)).

- Crime victim compensation is exempt (N.J. Stat. Ann. § 52:4B-18).

Please note that these exemptions are subject to change. It is essential to consult with a qualified bankruptcy attorney to ensure you are using the most up-to-date information and properly applying the exemptions to your specific situation.

Summary

Bankruptcy exemptions are a critical component of the bankruptcy process, allowing you to protect and retain essential assets during your financial recovery. By understanding the concept of exemptions, the differences between federal and state exemptions, and the process for claiming them, you can effectively navigate the bankruptcy process and preserve your property. Working with a knowledgeable bankruptcy attorney can help ensure that you maximize the available exemptions and protect as many of your assets as possible, setting the stage for a more stable financial future.

It is important to remember that exemptions are designed to give you a fresh start, not to leave you destitute or without the means to support yourself and your family. With a clear understanding of the exemptions available to you and the guidance of an experienced attorney, you can successfully navigate the bankruptcy process and emerge with the foundation necessary to rebuild your finances and move forward toward a more secure and prosperous future.

CHAPTER 14

Reaffirming Debt

▌▌ *The only man who sticks closer to you in adversity than a friend is a creditor."*

Reaffirming Debts – Choosing to Keep Specific Obligations

In some cases, you may wish to keep certain debts, such as a mortgage or car loan, even after filing for bankruptcy. Reaffirming a debt is a legal process that allows you to do so, effectively excluding the debt from the bankruptcy discharge and maintaining your obligation to repay it. This chapter will explore the concept of reaffirming debts, the reasons why you might choose to reaffirm, the process of reaffirmation, and the potential risks involved.

What is Reaffirmation?

Reaffirmation is a voluntary agreement between you, the debtor, and a creditor to continue paying a debt that would otherwise be discharged in bankruptcy. By reaffirming a debt, you agree to remain personally liable for repaying it, even after your bankruptcy discharge. In return, the creditor agrees not to repossess or foreclose on the property if you continue making payments as agreed.

Reasons to Reaffirm a Debt

Debtors typically choose to reaffirm secured debts, such as mortgages or car loans, for various reasons, including:

1. **Keeping the Property:** If you want to keep your home or vehicle and can afford the payments, reaffirming the debt can prevent the creditor from repossessing or foreclosing on the property.

2. **Maintaining a Positive Credit History:** Timely payments on reaffirmed debts can contribute to rebuilding your credit after bankruptcy, as the creditor may continue to report your payments to the credit bureaus.

3. **Negotiating Better Terms:** Reaffirmation may provide an opportunity to negotiate more favorable terms with the creditor, such as a reduced interest rate or extended repayment period.

The Reaffirmation Process

To reaffirm a debt, you must follow these steps:

1. **Identify the Debt:** Determine which debt(s) you wish to reaffirm and discuss the decision with your bankruptcy attorney to ensure it is in your best interest.

2. **Reaffirmation Agreement:** The creditor will prepare a reaffirmation agreement outlining the terms of the debt, including the balance, interest rate, and repayment terms.

3. **Review and Sign the Agreement:** Review the agreement with your attorney to ensure it accurately reflects the negotiated terms and is in your best interest. If you agree to the terms, sign the agreement.

4. **File the Agreement:** The reaffirmation agreement must be filed with the bankruptcy court before issuing your discharge.

5. **Court Approval:** In some cases, the bankruptcy court may require a hearing to determine whether the reaffirmation agreement is in your best interest and whether you can afford the payments. If the court approves the agreement, the reaffirmation becomes binding.

Risks of Reaffirming Debts

Reaffirming a debt is not without risks. It is crucial to consider these potential downsides before deciding to reaffirm:

Personal Liability: By reaffirming a debt, you remain personally liable for repaying it, even after your bankruptcy discharge. If you fail to make payments, the creditor can repossess or foreclose on the property and potentially sue you for any deficiency balance.

2. **Financial Burden:** Reaffirming a debt may create additional financial strain, making it more challenging to rebuild your finances after bankruptcy.

3. **Loss of Bankruptcy Protection:** If you reaffirm a debt and later encounter financial difficulties, you cannot include the reaffirmed debt in a subsequent bankruptcy filing for a certain period.

Summary

Reaffirming a debt can be a strategic decision that allows you to keep essential assets, maintain a positive credit history, and potentially negotiate better terms with your creditors. However, it is essential to carefully weigh the benefits and risks of reaffirming a debt and to consult with your bankruptcy attorney to ensure that the decision is in your best interest. By understanding the reaffirmation process and its potential consequences, you can make informed choices about which debts to reaffirm and effectively navigate the bankruptcy process. Ultimately, reaffirming a debt can be a valuable tool for some individuals, but it should be approached with caution and a clear understanding of your financial situation and future goals.

CHAPTER 15

Debt Management Courses

> ❚❚ *If you think nobody cares if you're alive, try missing a couple of car payments." - Earl Wilson*

The Debt Management Courses - A Crucial Step in the Bankruptcy Process

As part of the bankruptcy process, debtors must complete two debt management courses, one before filing their petitions and another after filing. These courses, also known as credit counseling and debtor education, are designed to help you understand the bankruptcy process, make informed decisions, and acquire the financial skills needed to manage your money effectively and avoid future financial problems.

This chapter will focus on both required courses, their objectives, and the completion process, including the option to take them online.

Pre-Filing Credit Counseling Course

Before filing for bankruptcy, you are required to complete a credit counseling course from an approved provider. This course aims to:

1. Evaluate your financial situation.

2. Help you understand the bankruptcy process and alternatives to bankruptcy.

3. Assist you in developing a personalized budget plan.

4. Discuss the potential consequences of filing for bankruptcy.

Upon completion of the course, you will receive a certificate that must be filed with the bankruptcy court when submitting your petition. The course must be completed within 180 days before filing your bankruptcy case.

Post-Filing Debtor Education Course

After filing your bankruptcy petition and before receiving a discharge, you must complete a debtor education course, also known as a financial management course, from an approved provider. The objectives of this course include:

1. Teaching you how to create and maintain a budget.

2. Providing information on using credit responsibly.

3. Offering strategies for managing money and rebuilding your credit after bankruptcy.

4. Emphasizing the importance of saving and investing for your future.

Upon completion of the second course, you will receive another certificate that also must be filed with the bankruptcy court to obtain your discharge. It is essential to complete the course promptly, as failure to do so may result in the dismissal of your bankruptcy case.

Taking the Courses Online

Both the pre-filing credit counseling and post-filing debtor education courses can be taken online, providing a convenient option for individuals with busy schedules or limited access to in-person courses. Your attorney will assist you in setting up and scheduling the courses. That said, all online courses must be taken with an approved provider to be valid. The U.S. Trustee Program maintains a list of approved credit counseling and debtor education providers on its website. If your provider is not approved for use, your petition may be rejected.

Summary

The required debt management courses are mandatory but provide valuable information and financial education to help you make informed decisions and achieve long-term financial stability. By completing both the pre-filing credit counseling and post-filing debtor education courses, you fulfill essential requirements of the bankruptcy process and set the foundation for a successful financial future. Taking these courses online offers a convenient and flexible option, allowing you to meet your obligations while balancing other personal and professional commitments.

CHAPTER 16

Discharge

"It always seems impossible until it is done." –
Nelson Mandela

The Bankruptcy Discharge - A Fresh Start and Conclusion of the Bankruptcy Process

The bankruptcy discharge is the ultimate goal and primary benefit of filing for bankruptcy. This discharge releases you from personal liability for certain debts, effectively wiping the slate clean and providing a fresh financial start. This chapter will discuss the bankruptcy discharge, the types of debts it covers, the timing of the discharge, and the conclusion of the bankruptcy process.

The Bankruptcy Discharge

When you receive a bankruptcy discharge, you are no longer legally obligated to pay most of the debts listed in your bankruptcy petition. The discharge prevents creditors from taking further collection actions against you for the discharged debts, including phone calls, letters, lawsuits, wage garnishments, or bank levies.

Debts Covered by the Bankruptcy Discharge

The bankruptcy discharge typically covers unsecured debts, such as:

1. Credit card debts

2. Medical bills

3. Personal loans

4. Utility bills

5. Certain older tax debts

However, not all debts are dischargeable in bankruptcy. Some non-dischargeable debts include:

1. Most student loans

2. Child support and alimony obligations

3. Recent tax debts

4. Debts incurred through fraud, embezzlement, or larceny

5. Court-ordered fines and restitution

6. Debts not listed in your bankruptcy petition

Timing of the Bankruptcy Discharge

In a Chapter 7 bankruptcy, you can generally expect to receive your bankruptcy discharge within 60 to 90 days after the Meeting of Creditors (341 Meeting). However, the discharge may be delayed or denied if:

1. You have not completed the required debtor education course.

2. A creditor or the trustee objects to the discharge of a specific debt or your entire bankruptcy case.

3. You have not adequately disclosed all your assets or provided accurate information in your bankruptcy petition.

Conclusion of the Bankruptcy Process

Once you receive your bankruptcy discharge, the bankruptcy process is nearly complete. The bankruptcy trustee will finalize the administration of your case, which may include selling any nonexempt assets and distributing the proceeds to your creditors. Once the trustee has completed these tasks, the bankruptcy court will issue a final decree, officially closing your bankruptcy case.

It is essential to keep a copy of your bankruptcy discharge and final decree for your records, as these documents prove that your debts have been discharged and your case has been closed.

With the discharge in hand and your case closed you can begin rebuilding your credit, reestablishing your financial stability, and moving forward with the knowledge and tools necessary to maintain a healthy financial future.

CHAPTER 17

Life After Bankruptcy

"Every moment is a fresh beginning." — T.S. Eliot

Rebuilding Your Financial Future

Emerging from bankruptcy presents a unique opportunity to regain control of your financial life and lay the foundation for a brighter future. Although bankruptcy can have a significant impact on your credit and financial standing, it is not the end of the road. By adopting responsible financial habits and making informed decisions, you can rebuild your credit, establish a sustainable budget, and pave the way for lasting financial success. This chapter will explore life after bankruptcy, focusing on rebuilding your credit, creating and maintaining a budget, and strategies for financial success.

Rebuilding Your Credit

The impact of bankruptcy on your credit can be daunting, but it is essential to remember that rebuilding your credit is a gradual process that requires patience and dedication. Consider the following steps to help rebuild your credit after bankruptcy:

1. **Review your credit reports:** Obtain a copy of your credit reports from the three major credit bureaus (Equifax, Experian, and TransUnion) and ensure that all discharged debts are accurately reported as "discharged" or "included in bankruptcy."

2. **Establish new credit:** Apply for a secured credit card or a credit-builder loan to establish a new line of credit. Make sure to keep your credit utilization low and pay your bills on time and in full.

3. **Pay bills on time:** Consistently paying your bills on time is crucial for rebuilding your credit, as payment history is a significant factor in your credit score.

4. **Monitor your progress:** Regularly check your credit reports and scores to track your progress and ensure accuracy.

Creating and Maintaining a Budget

Developing and adhering to a budget is critical to managing your finances and preventing future financial challenges. Consider the following steps to create and maintain a budget:

1.

Identify your income: Calculate your total monthly income, including wages, benefits, and any other sources of income.

2. **List your expenses:** Categorize and list all your monthly expenses, including fixed expenses (e.g., rent, mortgage, insurance) and variable expenses (e.g., groceries, utilities, entertainment).

3. **Set spending limits:** Assign a spending limit for each expense category, ensuring that your total expenses do not exceed your total income.

4. **Track your spending:** Regularly track your spending to ensure you stay within your budget. Adjust your spending limits as necessary.

5. **Review and adjust:** Periodically review your budget and make adjustments to accommodate changes in your financial circumstances or goals.

Strategies for Financial Success

Achieving financial success after bankruptcy requires a proactive approach and a commitment to making responsible financial decisions. Consider the following strategies:

1. **Build an emergency fund:** Set aside a portion of your income to build an emergency fund, aiming for three to six months' worth of living expenses.

2.

Prioritize debt repayment: Focus on repaying any remaining debts, prioritizing those with the highest interest rates.

3. **Save for retirement:** Contribute to a retirement account, such as a 401(k) or IRA, to ensure long-term financial security.

4. **Set financial goals:** Establish short-term and long-term financial goals, such as saving for a down payment on a home or paying off a student loan, and develop a plan to achieve them.

5. **Seek professional advice:** Consider working with a financial advisor or credit counselor to develop a personalized financial plan and receive guidance on managing your finances.

Summary

Life after bankruptcy offers a chance to reset your financial life and build a solid foundation for the future. By focusing on rebuilding your credit, creating and maintaining a budget, and implementing strategies for financial success, you can overcome the challenges of bankruptcy and move toward a more stable and prosperous future. Remember, the road to financial recovery may be long, but with patience, dedication, and informed decision-making, you can achieve lasting financial success.

As you navigate life after bankruptcy, you must remain vigilant about your financial habits and stay committed to your goals. Take the lessons you've learned from your bankruptcy experience and use them to foster a renewed sense of financial responsibility. Surround yourself with a support system, including friends, family, and financial professionals, to help keep you on track and motivated to make positive changes in your financial life.

Ultimately, remember that bankruptcy is not a life sentence but rather an opportunity to regain control of your financial situation and start anew. With the right mindset and a proactive approach, you can transform your financial future and live free from the burdens of debt.

Glossary of Bankruptcy Terms

Automatic Stay: A legal injunction which temporarily halts most collection activities, including lawsuits, wage garnishments, and creditor calls, once a bankruptcy petition is filed.

Bankruptcy: A legal process through which individuals or businesses seek relief from their debts by reorganizing or discharging them under the protection of federal bankruptcy laws.

Bankruptcy Code: Federal laws governing the bankruptcy process in the United States, codified under Title 11 of the United States Code.

Bankruptcy Court: The specialized federal court that handles bankruptcy cases and proceedings.

Bankruptcy Discharge: The court order that releases a debtor from personal liability for specific debts, effectively eliminating the debtor's legal obligation to pay them.

Bankruptcy Estate: The debtor's property and assets that become part of the bankruptcy case and are subject to administration by the bankruptcy trustee.

Bankruptcy Trustee: An impartial individual appointed by the bankruptcy court to administer a bankruptcy case, represent the interests of the creditors, and ensure the debtor complies with the Bankruptcy Code.

Chapter 7 Bankruptcy: A type of bankruptcy that involves liquidating non-exempt assets to repay creditors and discharge eligible debts.

Chapter 11 Bankruptcy: A type of bankruptcy that allows businesses and certain individuals to reorganize their debts and propose a repayment plan while continuing to operate.

Chapter 12 Bankruptcy: A type of bankruptcy designed for family farmers and fishermen, which allows them to reorganize their debts and propose a repayment plan.

Chapter 13 Bankruptcy: A type of bankruptcy that allows individuals with regular income to reorganize their debts and propose a repayment plan, typically lasting three to five years.

Creditor: A person or entity to whom the debtor owes money or has a legal obligation.

Debtor: An individual or entity that files for bankruptcy protection.

Debt Management Course: A required course for individuals filing bankruptcy that focuses on personal financial management and must be completed before receiving a bankruptcy discharge.

Dischargeable Debt: A type of debt that can be eliminated through the bankruptcy process, such as credit card debt, medical bills, and personal loans.

Exemptions: Specific types of property or assets that are protected from liquidation during the bankruptcy process, as determined by federal or state law.

Means Test: A financial assessment used in Chapter 7 bankruptcy cases to determine if the debtor's income is low enough to qualify for a discharge.

Non-Dischargeable Debt: A type of debt that cannot be eliminated through the bankruptcy process, such as student loans, certain tax debts, and child or spousal support obligations.

Petition: The official document filed with the bankruptcy court to initiate a bankruptcy case.

Pre-Bankruptcy Credit Counseling: A required course that must be completed before filing for bankruptcy, which aims to help individuals evaluate their financial situation and explore alternatives to bankruptcy.

Reaffirmation Agreement: A voluntary agreement between a debtor and a creditor that allows the debtor to continue paying a specific debt despite bankruptcy, typically used for secured debts like car loans or mortgages.

Secured Debt: A debt that is backed by collateral, such as a mortgage or car loan, which allows the creditor to repossess the property if the debtor fails to make payments.

Unsecured Debt: A debt that is not backed by collateral, such as credit card debt or medical bills.

341 Meeting (Meeting of Creditors): A mandatory meeting during the bankruptcy process where the debtor, the trustee, and any interested creditors can ask questions and review the debtor's financial situation.

Biographical note

About the Firm

The **Law Offices of Peter J. Lamont** is a premier, top-rated Bankruptcy, Real Estate, Business, Contracts, and Litigation law firm, serving all of New Jersey. Our primary office is conveniently located in Wyckoff, NJ, Bergen County. We recognize that every client, bankruptcy, lawsuit, real estate closing, and contract is different, which is why we offer a unique and individualized approach to solving our client's legal issues. Our focus is on what is best for our clients. We listen to the needs of every client and offer the best advice for each situation.

Our client relationships are built on trust and mutual respect and are advanced by outstanding communication and a truly collaborative working relationship. As a result, we have extremely high client retention rates. In fact, many of our clients have been with us for over 20 years.

Our top-rated attorneys and legal team combine knowledge of the law and years of experience with an unparalleled desire to provide our clients with outstanding client services. As a result, our clients receive the focus, attention, and results they deserve.

Bankruptcy Practice

The Fresh Start You Deserve

At the Law Offices of Peter J. Lamont, our experienced bankruptcy attorneys are dedicated to helping you get a fresh start through Chapter 7 bankruptcy. We understand that financial hardships can be overwhelming, but our team is here to guide you through every step of the process, from evaluating your eligibility to filing the necessary paperwork and representing you in court. Our primary goal is to ensure that you receive the maximum debt relief possible while preserving as many of your assets as we can. By thoroughly analyzing your financial situation and strategizing the best approach, we will work tirelessly to help you achieve a debt-free future. Let us help you regain control of your finances and rebuild your credit with the fresh start that Chapter 7 bankruptcy can provide.

Compassionate Support and Personalized Solutions

At our firm, we understand that facing financial difficulties can be an emotionally draining experience. Our team of caring and empathetic legal professionals is committed to making the bankruptcy process as seamless and stress-free as possible for you. We believe that by providing compassionate guidance and understanding, we can help alleviate some of the burden accompanying financial hardships. Our approach goes beyond simply offering legal assistance; we take the time to truly listen to your concerns and provide personalized solutions tailored to your unique circumstances. Our goal is not only to help you navigate the complexities of bankruptcy but also to ensure that you feel supported and understood throughout the entire process. By choosing our firm, you can be confident that you have a team of empathetic professionals by your side dedicated to helping you regain control of your finances and move towards a brighter future.

Holistic Legal Solutions for Complex, Interconnected Financial Issues

Often, bankruptcy matters are closely linked to various other concerns you might face, such as divorce, child support, taxes, or other legal disputes. Our skilled attorneys at the firm are well-equipped to help you address these interconnected issues. With our emphasis on integrity, confidentiality, and affordability, we will work collaboratively as your dedicated team to safeguard your interests and effectively resolve the underlying challenges.

About Peter J. Lamont, Esq.

Peter is the firm founder and a nationally recognized bankruptcy, business, contract, real estate, and litigation attorney. Over the past 20 years, Peter has represented businesses of all sizes and has served as general counsel for large international corporations. Peter has also helped thousands of people and businesses throughout New Jersey to buy and sell residential and commercial real estate.

Peter is a frequent speaker and lecturer at various corporate and community events and has been featured and interviewed by NPR, Fox, ABC, Dateline, and various other news and media publications. He also served as a contributing editor for Architectural Lighting Magazine, where he penned a monthly business practices column, and has written for Kitchen & Bath Business and other publications, including New Jersey Lawyer, Claims Magazine, and many more.

Peter spent his early career working for two large Wall Street law firms. While he appreciated the high level of legal work at these firms, he wanted better client communication and involvement. After years on Wall Street, Peter moved his practice to New Jersey and became a partner at a mid-sized New Jersey law firm, where he focused his practice on his business litigation, insurance defense, real estate, and representing large international corporations throughout the United States and Canada. Eventually, Peter decided that while he valued the experience of working with partners, he wanted complete control over his practice and how he worked and interacted with his clients. As a result, the Law Offices of Peter J. Lamont was born.

Peter is laser-focused on providing practical legal and business advice to his clients. Peter takes great pride in understanding his client's needs and end goals and devising a plan that provides them with the most practical, efficient, and cost-effective solutions possible. In 2012, Peter was one of the first lawyers to start a podcast called Understanding the Law Radio, or UTLRadio. Peter is admitted to the following Courts: United States Bankruptcy Courts, United States Court of Appeals for the Third Circuit, United States District Court, and New Jersey State Courts.

If you would like more information about Chapter 7 bankruptcy, please feel free to contact Peter. Contact information is available at www.pjlesq.com.

Made in the USA
Monee, IL
03 January 2025

75979508R00049